The Write Stuff: A *Style Manual for Effective Business Writing*

Written by Richard Andersen and
Helene Hinis
Edited by National Press Publications

NATIONAL PRESS PUBLICATIONS
A Division of Rockhurst College Continuing Education Center, Inc.
6901 West 63rd Street • P.O. Box 2949 • Shawnee Mission, Kansas 66201-1349
1-800-258-7246 • 1-913-432-7757

The Write Stuff: A Style Manual for Effective Business Writing
Published by National Press Publications, Inc.
© 1990 National Press Publications, Inc.

Printed in the United States of America

7   8   9   10

ISBN 1-55852-037-6

Table of Contents

1

MAKE YOUR WORDS TALK

"Man does not live by words alone, but he sometimes has to eat them." — Adlai Stevenson

Everything you write is a chance to make a good impression. If your writing contains mistakes, your readers will think you are careless or illiterate. If it is filled with jargon, your readers will think you are lazy or incapable of saying what you mean. If what you write is not easy to read, your readers will think your mind is not clear about what you want to say. Clear writing is the sign of a clear mind, and those who capture their ideas on paper stand out as fluent, confident and persuasive.

Think Differently About Yourself

Few things improve writing as much as a change in attitude. Think of yourself as a writer. Regardless of the kind of work you do, you are a writer. Your job is to communicate information and inspire people to act.

However, don't be a writer with a capital "W" — the kind that knows everything there is to know about writing except how to enjoy it. In other words, take your subject seriously but take yourself with a grain of salt. If you don't, your tone will sound hollow, your sentences will attract mold, and your reader's mind will blur with all the *of*'s and *which*'s you've used.

Care about the economy and beauty of clear, straightforward prose. Try not to lose your personality in the monotone of what you've been taught to admire as "professional." Consider this example of what many people consider good professional writing:

> The general problem is perhaps correctly stated
> as the inadequacy of nursing personnel to understand
> the demands of nursing services. Inadequacy is both
> a quantitative and a qualitative term and can in-
> dicate the insufficient numbers of nursing person-
> nel recruited to meet the demands for service.

What's the writer saying? Could you understand these two sentences after reading them once? Wouldn't it have been clearer if you had been told that there just aren't enough good nurses to go around? If you had to read that paragraph twice, so would most readers. Chances are you didn't even read it once — you just skimmed your way through to what you're reading now. If your writing is similar to that of the example paragraph, your readers will respond the same way you did. That means you'll spend time correcting the mistakes that come from their not having read your message, or you'll be on the phone answering questions about what you meant to say. Either way, you've lost time and energy that could have been devoted to other tasks.

Think Differently About Your Readers

The trouble with most business memos and letters is that they stick too close to the same standard: "In reference to your letter of . . . ," "Enclosed herewith . . . ," "Pursuant to our telephone conversation . . ." Who are these people that we say the same words to over and over again? Don't they have personalities that should reflect themselves in our language?

Writing is communication. When your writing fails to meet your readers' needs, you've failed to communicate. A clear sense of whom you are writing to is critical for successful communication. Organize and present your ideas with a targeted reader in mind. Don't be satisfied with putting down data and results or observations and opinions. Find a way to make this information meaningful to your reader.

This doesn't mean that you should talk down to your readers, however. When you lower yourself to what you think might be your readers' level, you actually insult them. You think you're being humble, but you may come across as arrogant.

Think of your readers as being just as intelligent and sincere about their jobs as you are. Even if they aren't, they'll appreciate your assuming they are. Respect for your readers goes a long way toward helping them see you as intelligent, reasonable and well-informed. Try to imagine what they might ask you, what they might object to, what they might already know, and what they might find interesting.

Think Differently About Your Subject

Show enthusiasm for your message. Studies show that readers respond positively to memos and letters that contain a sense of the writer's enthusiasm. They're encouraged to feel the time they spend reading the message is worthwhile.

This doesn't mean, however, that you should announce your excitement about a particular subject. Let the subject speak for itself, but choose words that convey your sense of enthusiasm. Expressions such as "without equal," "the most important factor," and "strongly recommend" show the reader that you're moved by the significance of your subject.

2

WRITING FOR STYLE

"I never write 'metropolis' for seven cents because I can get the same price for 'city.' I never write 'policeman' because I can get the same money for 'cop.'"
— Mark Twain

Your style is the way you say and do things. It's what makes you who you are, what separates you from everyone else and identifies you as you. In the same way that you have your own particular way of speaking and acting, you also have your own writing style. Or you should have.

Unfortunately, most of us don't know what our individual writing styles are because we were never given opportunities to discover them. Instead, we were taught to imitate other people's styles. First our teachers' and later our bosses' style.

To help you write in the same voice you would use when you speak, consider the following suggestions:

1. Don't write any word that you wouldn't say. "Perusal," "Pursuant to," and "As per your request" are examples of this kind of writing.

2. Don't substitute the impersonal "one" for "you," "we" or "I." When we speak, we rarely say "one must" or "one should"; we say "I must" and "you should."

3. Use contractions. Because we often speak in contractions, they are a subtle but effective way to draw readers into our messages and present ourselves as warm, accessible, friendly human beings.

Now this doesn't mean you should write *exactly* like you talk. Remember that you have many different speaking voices. You speak one way to your children and another way to your parents; one way to your bosses and another way *about* your bosses. If you're writing to a colleague, write in the voice you would use when speaking to that colleague. When writing to a boss or supervisor, write in the voice you would use when speaking to that boss or supervisor. That way, you'll always write in your own natural writing voice, yet maintain the professional tone or standard level of English that your memos and letters are expected to have.

3

EDITING FOR STYLE

"I may be the world's worst writer, but I'm the world's best rewriter." — James Michener

Good writers know that writing in their own voices only sounds good. The best writing comes from rewriting, and good writers spend more time rewriting than anything else. Their goal is to create carefully constructed prose that never loses the *illusion* of natural speech.

By writing frequently in your natural speaking voice, you will develop your own writing style. By rewriting what you write, you will retain the energy and power of your natural voice with all the hems, haws and digressions cut out.

After you've finished writing a memo or a letter, ask yourself these questions:

- **Is It Easy to Understand?** Does it say what I want to say in a simple, clear, straightforward way?

- **Does It Get to the Point?** Most of the time, the sooner we get to the point, the better.

- **Does It Stick to the Point?** Does the memo or letter remain faithful to my stated purpose? Have I kept the reader's needs continually in view? Are all my points clearly illustrated?

- **Is It Organized in a Logical Way?** Does my opening sentence focus the reader's attention in the direction I want him or her to go? Does each sentence build in some way on the one that came before it? Are there any illogical surprises? Does material need to be added, moved or omitted? To begin answering these questions, proofread your memo or letter from the reader's point of view. Ask yourself, "What's in this for the reader? Why should the reader agree with me?"

- **Does It Contain Any Unnecessary Words?** The more words we can eliminate in our writing, the more power we preserve. Consider how many words the writer of the following paragraph uses to tell people to start showing up on time for work:

    > It has been recently brought to our attention that many people are beginning to show up past the designated arrival times. This is not pursuant to company policy. Try to leave yourself enough time when you leave your homes in the morning to reach work by the arrival times that the personnel department has established as appropriate for your division.

- **Is It Complete?** Does it contain all the information the reader *needs* to know? Not every reader needs to know *all* the information that exists on any one subject.

• **Is It Positive?** Many times we disagree not with the opinion but with the way it is presented. Try not to be patronizing or condescending to your reader. See if you can present the negative in a positive or at least a neutral light. Instead of focusing on what your company rejects, emphasize what it approves of. Studies show that readers respond better to "Be on time" than "Don't be late." "We are unable to use your proposal" doesn't hit the reader with nearly the same force as "We are not going to use your proposal." Which would you rather be told: "Your letter reads easily, but there are several things you failed to include" or "Your letter reads easily, and here are a couple of things you can do to make your next letter even more effective"?

• **Is It Accurate?** Have you exaggerated anything, been unfair in any way, or failed to distinguish between fact and interpretation? If you do anything to break your reader's trust, your reader will never trust you again.

• **Does It Flow?** Is it easy to read even if the subject is complex? Does the information get in the way of understanding? The more complicated the information, the shorter the sentences should be.

• **Does the Opening Grab My Attention?** If you don't have your readers' attention in the first five to 10 seconds, their attention will drift. To grab your readers' attention and make them want to continue:

  1. *Make a point up front.* Tell the reader what your message is about in the opening line.

  2. *State the good news.* Tell the reader what he or she wants to hear most. Put what benefits the reader right at the beginning.

3. **Ask a question.** When your reader answers it, he or she will be participating in your letter right from the start.

4. **Present a gripping fact.** Don't just state the information; present it in a way that's meaningful to the reader. Compare "Earnings were down .7% in the last quarter" with "If we don't start making a profit soon, the photocopy machine will have to be monitored, outside telephone lines will have to be restricted and those in sales will have to pay for their own postage."

• **Is It Correct?** Although words and the ways they are used can change, most standards of meaning and usage remain the same. Even if your writing is clear, logical, precise and attention-grabbing, you will undermine your credibility with the reader if your choice of words is not consistently correct and appropriate.

Consider, for example, the word "boss." Dictionaries define "boss" as an employer or supervisor of workers. Given this definition, it is correct to refer to a supervisor as a "boss." Given the negative connotations often associated with the word, however, "boss" rarely appears in business writing. The definition may be correct, but in this context the word is inappropriate.

Make mistakes such as this and your readers will think you are either careless or uneducated. They will respond the same way for errors in spelling, punctuation and grammar. Try to make everything you write as close to perfect as you can.

4

PARAGRAPHS

*"When I see a paragraph shrinking under my eyes
like a strip of bacon, I know I'm on the right track."*
— Peter DeVries

Paragraphs are like rest stops. They give our eyes and mind a break. They tell us we've just come to the end of something and can take a breath before going on to the next matter.

In grammar school, we were taught that every paragraph has to have a beginning, a middle and an end. Today, paragraphs can be any length. They can be as short as one sentence or even one word. One-word paragraphs make very powerful paragraphs.

Right?

Instead of thinking of paragraphs as having beginnings, middles and ends, consider good paragraphs as having:

Unity. Try to stick to one idea to each paragraph and place that idea in the opening sentence. This lets your reader know what your paragraph is about and the attitude he or she should have toward your subject. The concluding sentence of your paragraph should lead your reader into the opening sentence of the paragraph that follows.

Coherence. "Coherence" comes from the Latin word meaning "to stick together." Paragraph coherence means that the sentences in the paragraph connect. Each is in some way tied to the one that came before it. To create coherent paragraphs:

1. *Arrange the sentences in a logical pattern or order.* The order may be one of time, space, size, importance, general to specific, or similarity and difference.

2. *Keep a consistent point of view.* Avoid shifting from one person to another, from one tense to another, or from singular to plural without good reason. Consider beginning a new paragraph for every shift in person, tense and number.

3. *Repeat key words or phrases.* Or use synonyms. This keeps the reader's attention focused where you want it.

4. *Use transitional words or phrases.* Transitional words help the reader get from one idea to the next.

   • Words that indicate *addition* include: again, also, and, and then, besides, further, furthermore, moreover, in addition.

   • Words that indicate *order* are: first, second, third, next, finally.

   • Words that indicate *summary* are: in brief, in short, in conclusion.

- Words that indicate *example* are: for example, for instance, in particular.

- Words that indicate *result* are: as a result, consequently, therefore, then, thus, so, for this reason.

- Words that indicate *comparison* include: similarly, in the same way as, more than, less than.

- Words that indicate *contrast* include: however, nevertheless, on the other hand, yet, unlike, but, despite, in spite of.

- Words that indicate *time* include: afterward, immediately, meanwhile, soon, now, at last, presently, shortly.

Emphasis. Begin and end each paragraph with important pieces of information and well-written sentences. This will make your reader want to continue from one paragraph to the next.

Here are some examples of the kinds of opening sentences that help maintain a reader's attention:

- *Name the person or audience you are addressing.* This almost always catches the reader's attention and directs it to the words that follow.

- *Begin with an answer to a question or opposing point of view* that may be raised in the reader's mind by something you said in your previous paragraph.

- *State the main idea of the paragraph in the opening sentence.* Follow with the reasons why it should or should not be supported.

- *Ask a question.* When the reader answers it, he or she is involved in your subject.

- *Make a prediction.* You can point to the consequences of a present situation by telling your reader what will happen if he or she doesn't act now.

- *Open with an appealing or amusing incident* that will arouse your reader's curiosity.

The closing sentence of each paragraph is the best place to form a link with the opening sentence of the next paragraph, but ask yourself if you need one. If each paragraph in your memo or letter develops a point in a series, you don't need to sum up what you've said before going on to the next paragraph. Unless the information is so important it merits repetition, end each paragraph with a transition that makes the reader want to hurry on to the next paragraph.

Here are some of the kinds of endings you can close your paragraphs with:

- Summarize the main point of the paragraph and introduce the reader to the point that will begin the next paragraph.

- Restate the paragraph's thesis if it was about something you hoped to prove.

- Direct the reader's attention to the possible consequences of a situation already presented in the paragraph.

- Call upon the reader to act, or tell the reader what action you will take.

- End with a quotation that confirms the views presented in the paragraph.

The last line of the last paragraph of any memo or letter is almost as important as the opening one. Well-written endings give readers a sense of completeness. Their interest, which was aroused in the opening line and maintained in the opening lines of the subsequent paragraphs, should be satisfied in the concluding line of the last paragraph. To prevent disappointing your readers:

1. Do not introduce a new idea into the concluding line of your memo or letter. If it is important, incorporate it into the main body of what you've written.

2. Do not begin your last sentence with "In conclusion" or "To summarize." Well-written endings are self-evident.

3. Do not apologize for your opinions. You're entitled to them and, if they are substantially supported and carefully presented, won't require an admission of whatever inadequacies you might feel.

A Final Word About Paragraphs

Construct your paragraphs with a good eye as well as a good mind. Enormous blocks of print implant the image of a difficult subject in your readers' minds. Breaking a long paragraph in two, even if it isn't necessary, can be an important visual aid. On the other hand, a whole bunch of short paragraphs one right after the other can be distracting. The safest policy is to vary the length of your paragraphs without, of course, making the breaks seem forced or unnatural. Few things irritate readers more than to pick up an attractive page of prose only to have sentences pulled out from under them when they least expect it.

Consider how the paragraph you just read looks on the page. Would it be more appealing to the eye to divide it into two paragraphs, with the second paragraph beginning "The safest policy is . . ."?

Now consider the paragraph above divided this way:

Construct your paragraphs with a good eye as well as a good mind.

Enormous blocks of print implant the image of a difficult subject in your readers' minds. Breaking a long paragraph into two, even if it isn't necessary, can be an important visual aid.

On the other hand, a whole bunch of short paragraphs one right after the other can be distracting.

The safest policy is to vary the length of your paragraphs without, of course, making the breaks seem forced or unnatural.

Few things irritate readers more than to pick up an attractive page of prose only to have sentences pulled out from under them when they least expect it.

Obviously, no rule governs the length of paragraphs. A paragraph should be as long or as short as is necessary to cover the idea presented in the paragraph. Generally speaking, however, the shorter the paragraphs and the fewer the number of ideas contained in them, the easier they are to read.

5

SENTENCES

*"Good writing is a kind of skating that carries off
the performer where he would not go."*
— Ralph Waldo Emerson

The most effective way to write lively, powerful, engaging
sentences is to write as close as possible to the way you speak.
In other words, be yourself. Once you have the energy of clear,
honest, natural words on paper, then you can forge them into the
kind of sentences that Ernest Hemingway says separate
architecture from interior decorating. Here are some tips on
how to do it:

Choose Nouns Over Adjectives. Adjectives are indispensable
to speech, but there isn't one that can replace even the weakest
noun. Nouns are where the information is. They're the names

of the people, places and things our readers want most to know about.

Adjectives drain most nouns of their color. Especially if they are overdone. The adjective "very," for example, is particularly debilitating: "This is a very important lesson that we should all pay very close attention to."

Choose Verbs Over Adverbs. Verbs are where the action is. They're the ones that give good writing its power. Although there is nothing wrong with adverbs, you preserve energy in a sentence every time you eliminate one or replace it and the verb it assists with a stronger verb. Consider the difference between "John went quickly to the photocopy machine" and "John rushed to the photocopy machine." The word "rushed" is doing more than twice the work of "went" and "quickly."

Choose Plain Words Over Fancy Ones. Let your ear be your guide. If you wouldn't say the word, you're probably better off not writing it. Rich, ornate, beauteous words are often unhealthy and sometimes sickening.

Choose Specific Words Over General Ones. One of the surest ways to hold any reader's attention is to be specific. The more specific you are, the sharper the pictures you create in your readers' minds, and the better they remember what you've said. Instead of telling your reader, "I'll call you next week about this problem," consider "Joan, I'll call you next Thursday afternoon about Bob's request for a raise. Let me know then what you want me to tell him." "I'll call you next week" is too vague. "I'll call you next Thursday afternoon," however, lets Joan know that Thursday afternoon she's going to hear from you. During the week, she's going to be thinking about that telephone call, and the chances are good that when you call she'll have some idea what she wants you to tell Bob.

Choose Short Sentences Over Long Sentences. Especially if the information is complicated. Some editors claim that any sentence with more than 17 words is too long, but there is no sure-fire rule governing the length of sentences. A sentence should be as short or as long as is necessary to express a complete thought. Generally speaking, short sentences are easier to read. On the other hand, beware of lining up too many short sentences in a row:

> I received your order for 25 office chairs on October 4. A labor strike has delayed shipment. We recently hired new workers. Your chairs will be on their way in a week. I apologize for the inconvenience. It won't happen again. Your patience is appreciated.

Choose the Personal Over the Impersonal. People enjoy reading and responding to other people. Instead of merely stating the benefits of a particular product, service or idea, show the reader how what you have to offer will benefit him or her in some specific, personal way. Say, for example, you want your client to renew his or her insurance policy. Instead of just pointing out how much money your client will be awarded under what circumstances, remind your client of the time he or she had an accident and how quickly your company responded. Or tell your client about the time something happened to another client and how you were able to help that person in ways other agents or insurance companies couldn't.

A Final Word About Sentences

Draw a slash through each period in every memo or letter you write. If the distance between the slashes is approximately the same, all your sentences are pretty much the same length; and if all your sentences are approximately the same length, you're putting your reader to sleep. Vary the length of your sentences the same way you would vary the length of your paragraphs: it is a subtle way to keep your readers awake.

6

PHRASES

"Style is the effectiveness of assertion."
— George Bernard Shaw

A phrase is a group of words that doesn't have a subject or a verb but gives meaning to a sentence:

> The insurance agent runs his business *from a computer in his living room.*

One of the first signs of insecure writers is the number of phrases they use to say what could be said in just a few words. Instead of writing "now" or "then," these writers hang on to "at this point in time." Not only do these phrases pad messages with unnecessary words, we've heard them before. Many times before.

Cliches

Phrases that unnecessarily lengthen messages and have been repeated so often as to become cliches work against us in two ways: they bore the reader and dehumanize the writer by substituting artificial voices for natural ones.

Nevertheless, we continue to put these prefabricated phrases into our memos and letters because we've learned to depend on them. They enable us to get some words on paper whenever we have a writing assignment. Phrases such as "In reference to your letter of . . ," "As per our telephone conversation of . . ," and "Enclosed herewith please find . . ," help us get started. Once we have these words down on paper, we've been given the momentum to add whatever other words are necessary to complete the opening paragraph. Then we search our stock of cliches for a way to open the second paragraph. The final line of our memos and letters ends with "If you have any questions concerning this matter, please do not hesitate to contact me."

Sound familiar? These phrases may help us begin paragraphs and end letters, but they also undermine whatever power our subject may have by numbing the reader's senses.

Use these phrases if you need them to get started. Then, once you've completed your memo or letter, go back and see how many of them you can eliminate, reword or place somewhere else in your message. If you feel you need the information contained in the prefabricated phrase, see if you can reword it. Instead of saying, "Pursuant to our agreement," for example, try "When we agreed to . . ."

Another problem with prefabricated phrases is that they are often too general or vague. That's why we can use them in so many different contexts. Unfortunately, they don't inspire our readers to act as quickly or as efficiently as specific instructions. "I look forward to your response regarding this matter" is not nearly effective as "Make sure those figures are on my desk by Tuesday at 10 o'clock."

Prepositional Phrases

Having eliminated as many cliches such as "In reference to . . ." "As per . . ." and "In accordance with . . ." as you can, look at your prepositional phrases. A prepositional phrase is a group of words introduced by a preposition. The preposition usually introduces a noun: "In the meeting room," "by the desk," or a pronoun: "to him," "for them." Most prepositional phrases are used as adjectives, "The subject of *the article on sales techniques* . . .," or adverbs, "He went *to New York to sign* the contract."

Prepositional phrases become a problem when you line up too many in a row. Notice how quickly your reading energy is drained by the parade of prepositional phrases in the following sentence: "The Danubian Basin changed rapidly under the impact *of forces within the core area of the rising economic system*."

Here's some advice for handling prepositional phrases:

Two prepositional phrases in a row: no problem.
Three in a row: think twice about it.
Four in a row: almost always a disaster.

If you write three or four consecutive prepositional phrases, see if you can spread the information they contain over several sentences. Or perhaps some of the information can be placed in another paragraph.

And speaking of prepositions . . . remember being told it's wrong to end a sentence in a preposition? Thanks to Winston Churchill, it's okay now to end sentences in a preposition. Once asked if he ever ended a sentence with a preposition, Churchill replied, "Ending a sentence with a preposition is something up with which I will not put." He made us realize the absurdity of this rule. If when you speak you end your sentences in a preposition, it's also acceptable to end your sentences with a preposition when you write.

A Final Word on Phrases

Phrases that have been around so long they've outlived their usefulness have no place in effective memos and letters. Combat their influence by allowing the meaning of your message to choose your words rather than the other way around.

When you think of a specific person, place or thing, a picture comes into your mind. If you want to describe that person, place or thing, search for the words that best express what you see in your mind. In other words, don't search for words that will create a mental picture. See the picture first, then describe it.

When you begin your messages with an abstract idea, you are more likely to have words in your mind rather than pictures. If you're not careful, these words will hinder your developing a clear mental picture. They may even change the meaning of what you want your readers to understand. For this reason, it is probably better to avoid thinking of words until you can visualize a picture of what you want to say. Then you can choose the words and phrases that best fit your meaning and make the best impression. This will help you see more clearly the stale or mixed images, the prefabricated phrases, and the unnecessary repetitions. Then, if you're still not sure about the effect of a particular word or phrase, consult author George Orwell's guidelines for clear writing:

1. Never use a word or phrase that you are used to seeing in print.

2. Never use a phrase where a word will do.

3. If it's possible to cut a phrase, cut it.

4. Never use a foreign or scientific word or phrase if you can think of an everyday English equivalent.

For additional advice on style, consult the following:

- **Associated Press Stylebook and Libel Manual.**
  The Associated Press.

- **The Chicago Manual of Style.**
  The University of Chicago Press.

- **Webster's Standard and American Style Manual.**
  Merriam-Webster, Inc.

- **The McGraw-Hill Style Manual.**
  McGraw-Hill Book Company.

- **The New York Times Manual of Style and Usage.**
  Times Books.

7

WORDS

"The small words work best and the old small words work best of all."

— Winston Churchill

Business writing is often cold, stiff and impersonal; and many business writers favor language that is pompous, archaic, trite and more formal than ordinary business situations require. Some favor the passive voice ("It has been brought to our attention . . .") over the active voice (We just learned . . ."), and begin too many of their sentences with "it" ("It has been decided . . ." or "It appears . . ."). If you write a sentence in the passive voice, try switching to the active voice. Can you see an improvement? If you begin a sentence with "it" and the "it" doesn't refer to something in the previous sentence, cross out the "it" and perhaps the two or three words that follow. See the difference it makes:

— *It has been recently brought to our attention that many people are showing up late for work.*

— *Many people are showing up late for work.*

The most effective words are the ones you say every day. When you speak on the phone or in person, you know the words that work and those that don't. You've already tested them. So why not put these proven words into your writing? Write the way you speak and your writing will be much more lively, powerful and engaging than if you write the way you *think* writing should sound.

Tone

Writing, like conversation, has *tone*. The tone of your writing and speaking voices expresses the attitude you have toward your subject. Tone can be personal or impersonal, formal or informal, positive or negative. The way in which you handle the tone of voice in your writing plays an important role in determining your reader's reaction to what you have to say.

Generally speaking, the more natural the tone of your writing voice, the more appealing your message will be. Consider the following two sentences:

1. It is to be observed that contracting for services provides the only means available to us to ensure timely compliance.

2. Unless we provide some of these services by contracting businesses outside our own, we won't finish the project on time.

The sentences have the same meaning and length, but the tone in each is different. The first sentence is pretentious, impersonal and difficult to read. The second is much closer to the way we speak.

Here are some examples of expressions that sound artificial compared with an improvement that sounds natural. Notice how the natural phrasings sound more sincere:

1. Allow me to express our appreciation for . . .
   Thank you for your help.

2. We wish to acknowledge receipt of . . .
   We have your . . .

3. With regard to your letter of . . .
   You say in your letter that . . .

Think of the people you like to hear from. Aren't they the ones who let their personalities come through regardless of their profession? The same is true for you. Your readers want to hear from the warm, genuine person they spoke to on the phone or met for lunch. So express yourself in writing the same way you speak. The more you are you, the more willing your readers will be to listen and to agree with what you have to say.

Here are some guidelines to help you get your message across without taking away anything from who you are:

Use Short Words. Long words slow the reader down. Look at the words on the left-hand side of each of the columns listed below. Compare how long it takes to say them with the speed of the words in the parentheses.

affirmative (yes) .... anticipate (expect)
cooperate (help) .... determine (find)
facilitate (make easy) ...... forward (send)
inasmuch as (since) .... indicate (show)
personnel (people) .... prior to (before)
pertaining to (about) .... presently (now)
request (ask) .... submit (give)
terminate (end) .... transpire (happen)

Use words such as the ones in the parentheses, and your readers will understand your messages faster, easier and with fewer chances of misinterpreting what you say.

Use Orthodox Spelling. Writing "nite" for "night," "thru" for "through," and "cuz" for "because" may be acceptable in a personal letter or for the name of a store trying to catch people's attention (Kopy Kat PhotoKopy), but it has no place in business letters or memos.

Use Necessary Words. Eliminate any word that does not contribute to your message. The more unnecessary words you can eliminate, the stronger and clearer your writing will be. Consider the following two sentences:

1. According to statistical data received by this office, there is an increasing amount of investment on the part of the government being made available for computer research.

2. The government is increasing its investment in computer research.

Both sentences convey the same meaning, but notice how much clearer, shorter and easier to read is the second.

Here are some phrases and their concise alternatives:

> at this point in time .... now
> for the purpose of .... to
> in the event that .... if
> due to the fact that .... because
> in the final analysis .... finally
> until such time as .... until

Use Personal Words. Until recently, using words such as "I" and "we" was considered bad form in business writing. The common substitute was the word "one." Today, with business writers moving toward greater directness and simplicity in their style, "I" and "we" are not only acceptable, they're encouraged.

Notice the difference between the awkward sentence that follows and the improved rewrite:

— If there are any problems regarding the above-mentioned matter, please direct all inquiries to the customer relations office.

— If you have any problems, please contact me.

On the other hand, you don't want to be too personal. Notice the difference between this overly informal sentence and the improved rewrite:

— You've got to remember that the main thing about taking minutes is getting them transcribed quickly.

— Please transcribe the meeting notes as soon as possible.

Notice, however, that even the wordy first example is preferable to the impersonal, detached, machine-like tone we've come to admire in most memos and letters as "professional." The best professional writing is somewhere in between. It achieves a sense of balance between the personal and the impersonal, the formal and the informal.

Use Contractions. Unless you want to maintain a strictly formal relationship with your reader, consider using contractions. Because contractions are spoken so naturally, they are a very subtle way to draw the reader into your message and allow you to come across as warm and personal.

Use Words That People Like to Hear. There are many words people like to hear in some contexts and others that they don't.

Positive-sounding words help create a positive response. Compare the words people like to hear in the column on the left with those that turn people off:

achieve .... blame
appreciate .... complain
success .... failure
you say .... you claim
can .... impossible
welcome .... won't

Use Speaking Words. Many writers feel they have to dress up ordinary words when they write. They want to sound learned and important, but they wind up sounding obscure and affected.

If you use pretentious-sounding word constructions such as those in the left-hand column, consider substituting the plain, simple words listed on the right:

heretofore .... before
to be in receipt of .... have
enclosed please find .... here is
commensurate with .... equal to
termination .... end

Use Correct Words. Words that mean what they say and say what they mean. Here are some commonly misused words and what you can do about them:

Affect, Effect. "Affect" is a verb. It means "to change" or "to influence." "Effect" can be a verb or a noun. As a verb it means "to cause"; as a noun, it means "a result."

Aggravate, Irritate. To "aggravate" is "to add to" something that is already troublesome; to "irritate" is "to annoy."

All right, Alright. "Alright" is not a word. You'd never write "alwrong," would you?

Allude, Elude. You "allude" or "make reference to" a book; you "elude" or "run away from" someone who is chasing you.

Alot. An "alot" is a camel. One thing we don't need in the office is a lot of "alots."

Among, Between. Use "among" when more than two are involved; use "between" when you are comparing two persons, places or things.

And/Or. A shortcut that looks and reads bad and can lead to confusion or ambiguity. Avoid whenever possible.

Anybody, Anyone. "Anybody" is written as one word when it refers to "any person." "Any body" as two words means "any corpse" or "any group." The same is true for "everybody," "nobody" and "somebody." "Anyone" means "anybody"; "any one" means "any single person" or "any single thing."

Assure, Ensure, Insure. To "assure" is "to speak confidently" about something; to "ensure" is "to make sure" or "to make certain"; to "insure" is "to protect something against loss or damage with an insurance policy."

Being. Not needed after "regard" in sentences such as "He was regarded as *being* the best." Preferred is "He was regarded as the best."

Can, May. "Can" means "able to"; "may" means "permit." "Can I leave work early?" means "Am I able to leave work early?" "Is all my work done?" "Are my legs strong enough to carry me out?" "May I leave work early?" means "May I have permission to go home early?"

Compare To, Compare With. To "compare to" is to point out the similarities in different things; to "compare with" is to point out the differences between similar things. Life can be *compared to* a rat race; rat races can be *compared with* rush-hour traffic.

Couldn't Care Less, Could Care Less. "Couldn't care less" means you care so little about something it would be impossible for you to care less. "Could care less" is an expression that comes from people not hearing the "n't" in "couldn't care less."

Data. Like "media" and "phenomena," "data" is plural. It refers to more than one fact or piece of evidence. Nevertheless, it is becoming popular to refer to it as singular. Your choice: "The data *is* misleading" or "The data *are* misleading."

Disability, Handicap. A "disability" is a physical or emotional impairment; a "handicap" occurs when a person cannot overcome his or her disability. A person in a wheelchair is handicapped in certain situations; a person who has learned to overcome a reading disability is no longer handicapped.

Disinterested, Uninterested. To be "disinterested" is to be "impartial," "fair" or "without prejudice"; to be "uninterested" is to be not interested.

Farther, Further. "Farther" has to do with distance: "I traveled *farther* than you." "Further" can be used to indicate distance, but it can also be used as a verb meaning "to promote" or "to advocate": "I plan to *further* your cause."

Finalize. Can mean either "to terminate" or "to put into final form." Avoid the word altogether. It's overused, pretentious and pseudo-technical; substitute "finish" or "complete."

Fewer, Less. "Fewer" has to do with numbers; "less" has to do with quantity.

* *Fewer* sales representatives spoke at this year's conference. (To use *less* here would mean the people were missing arms and legs.)
* People are smoking *less* and exercising more.

Gratuitous, Gratuity. Gratuitous means "undeserved" or "unearned"; a gratuity is a "tip for services rendered."

Hopefully. "Hopefully" used to mean "with hope"; now it means "I hope," and it drives office grammarians into fits of rage and exasperation. They reason that if you write "*Hopefully,* you will write your proposal on time," you don't know if you hope to write it or you are writing it in a hopeful frame of mind. These same people who crusade against the common use of "hopefully," however, see nothing wrong with saying, "*Admittedly, hopefully* is an obsession of mine."

I, Me. When our parents heard us say sentences such as "Bob and me played baseball," they told us to say "Bob and I." Because we were told so often to say "Bob and I," we tend to use "I" any time we join it with someone else's name. What's the best way to tell when to use "I" or "me"? Read the sentence without the other person's name.

Imply, Infer. They don't mean the same thing. To "imply" is to suggest or indicate without expressing exactly what you want to say: "He *implied* that we were going to get a raise." To "infer" is to reach a conclusion from the evidence at hand: "Based on what he said, we can *infer* that a raise will be coming."

Irregardless. No such word. The word we want is "regardless."

Its, It's. "Its" is the possessive form of "it." It means something belongs to whatever place or thing "it" stands for: "This computer is more expensive than most because *its* screen is so large and clear." "It's" is the contraction for "it is": "*It's* a large and clear screen."

-ize. So many good verbs end in "-ize," we don't need to add this tempting suffix to any more. Listen to what sounds natural (words in the column on the left) and what sounds pseudo-intellectual (words in the column on the right):

criticize	finalize
harmonize	prioritize
fraternize	departmentalize
fertilize	stylize

Like, As. Except as a term of affection, "like" has to do with comparison: "That was not *like* him." "As" can be used in comparisons ("The two were equally *as* efficient" or "He was *as* efficient *as* she," but it also appears as the introduction or heading of a list ("The program included such topics as: . . .").

Plan Ahead. Would you ever "plan behind"? Just "plan" is sufficient.

Reason Is Because, Reason Is That. "Reason is because" is considered redundant because both "reason" and "because" have to do with cause. "Reason is that" is the grammatically correct expression.

Secondly, Thirdly. If you wouldn't say "firstly" — and you shouldn't — stick to "first," "second," "third."

Thanking You in Advance. Unnecessary words. In all cases, the plain, simple, straightforward "thank you" is sufficient.

Try to, Try and. To "try to" is "to attempt." "To try and" implies that two separate actions are taking place: the "try" and whatever verb comes after it.

Unique. Because "unique" means "without equal," there can be no degrees of uniqueness, no "most unique" or "very unique."

Use Active Voice. Most of the time active voice is shorter, simpler, clearer, more direct and easier to understand than passive voice. Active voice moves readers along; passive voice slows them down.

Passive voice is the language of irresponsibility. Its purpose is to mislead, distort and disguise. Very rarely will a company announce in the active voice, "We made a mistake." Almost always, the company will state: "An error was found." Apparently, it was lying in the hall and somebody happened to trip over it.

There are reasons for using passive voice constructions. Most of the time, however, they are unnecessary.

Passive: The street was crossed by the chicken.

Active: The chicken crossed the street.

Active voice puts the chicken and the road where they belong.

To discover passive voice, look for the word "by." If the word "by" has a verb in front of it, you may have written something in the passive voice. See if it sounds better to change it to active. Almost everything we say is in the active voice.

Be Consistent. Maintain the same verb tense throughout each paragraph that you write. If you begin a paragraph in the present tense, stay in the present tense until you end the paragraph. Or if you want to switch tenses, begin a new paragraph with every tense change.

Avoid "Headline" Words. "Headline" words are words that newspaper editors have shortened for reasons of space. Many may be inappropriate outside of the newspaper. Here are some headline words and what you want to substitute for them:

GOP ....Republican Party
GM ....General Motors
America ....United States
Russia ....Soviet Union
UN ....United Nations
quote ....quotation
recap ....recapitulate

Avoid Cliches. Cliches are expressions that have been used so often they've lost whatever energy they might originally have had. Here are some cliches and words to consider using in their place:

tried and true....................reliable
the bottom line.................the deciding factor
don't hesitate to call ....please call
few and far between ....rare
in a nutshell ....in short
at this point in time ....now

Avoid Euphemisms. Euphemisms are words and phrases meant to hide negative things. Some of them — "deceased" for "dead," for example — have their place, but most of them dull our style and serve no useful role in business writing.

Euphemism......................Alternative
revenue enhancement ......price increases
negative impact ....bad effect
pre-owned ....used
contrary to expectations ..unexpected

Avoid Jargon. Use technical language or words peculiar to a special business when these words meet the needs of a particular reader. The rest of the time, write in plain, non-technical, conversational prose. Compare this sentence about computers, "Companies are increasingly turning to capacity planning techniques to determine when future processing loads will exceed processing capability," with "We're planning for the day when our computers run out of room."

Other jargon words include:

utilization	prioritization	interface
market penetration	impact (as a verb)	optimize
task (as a verb)	facilitated	economy measures

Avoid Redundancy. Redundant writers can't let any single word do its job. Just to make sure they don't miss the importance of the point they're trying to make, these writers find all kinds of ways to say everything twice. "Unanimous" becomes "completely unanimous." Here are some more commonly used redundancies and their corresponding sufficient meanings:

brief in duration	brief
during the year 1990	during 1990
resulting effect	effect
unresolved problem	problem
repeat the same	repeat
surplus left over	surplus
advance warning	warning
three-month period	three months

Redundancy doesn't help clarify meaning or enrich style. Nevertheless, the repetition of certain key words and phrases can reinforce important points and enhance eloquence:

The chief problem we face is increasing competition: competition from Japan, competition from Taiwan, competition from Korea, and competition from Germany.

Keep Related Words Together. Badly placed words and phrases can cause confusion in a sentence. Keep the words that have to do with a subject apart from those that do not have to do with that subject. Note in the following examples what the writers meant to say and what they actually said:

— In accordance with your instructions, I have sold my stock in the enclosed envelope.

— I have been in the office with this proposal for two weeks.

— The city's first sperm bank opened with semen samples from 18 men frozen in a stainless steel tank.

Avoid Acronyms, Initials and Abbreviations. Not everyone knows that SALT means Strategic Arms Limitation Talks. Write out the complete name the first time it is used and place the acronym, initials or abbreviations in parentheses following the name. Once you've given your readers their bearings, you can use the acronym, initials or abbreviation in place of the organization's name or the movement that you are writing about: "The National Association for the Advancement of Colored People (NAACP) will elect a new president this year."

Avoid Sexist Language. Words that favor one gender over the other have no place in business or any other kind of writing. Such language occurs mostly with the third-person masculine pronouns ("he," "him," "himself," "his") and with job titles that have a built-in gender preference ("foreman," "chairman," "stewardess").

To avoid sexist pronouns use the "he or she" construction ("Each manager must file his or her report.") or switch to the less awkward plural "they," "them, "their," "themselves" whenever possible ("All managers must file their reports."). Although still seen as incorrect by grammarians, the use of a plural "they" to refer to a singular subject is yet another option. Follow the guidelines and philosophy of your organization when determining which option is best.

To avoid sexist job titles, change to forms that have no gender:

mailman	letter carrier
salesman	sales representative
policeman	police officer
newsman	journalist
fireman	firefighter
chairman	chairperson
spokesman	spokesperson

Also change sexist words that aren't necessarily job titles:

mankind	people
manned	staffed
average man	average person
all men	all people

And don't forget to give men and women equal treatment:

men and ladies	men and women
man and wife	husband and wife
John Dow and Mary	John Dow and Mary Ward

If you still think "man" can stand for both men and women, consider this sentence:

Modern man no longer pampers himself during pregnancy. He works almost up until the day of delivery and is back at work within a few weeks of leaving the hospital.

Use a Thesaurus. But only to remember words, not to discover new ones. If we use the thesaurus to find big words that we can put in the place of little words, we risk distorting what we mean to say. If you've written a word and know there's a better word but can't remember what it is, reach for the thesaurus. Otherwise, most of the words you need to be a lively, powerful, engaging writer are in your mind and heart.

Use a Dictionary. To discover the meaning or correct spelling of a word, use a dictionary. The first definition listed is usually the preferred usage. Here is a list of commonly used dictionaries:

1. ***Webster's New World Dictionary, 3rd Edition.*** Simon and Schuster.

2. ***Random House College Dictionary.***   Random House.

3. ***American Heritage Dictionary.***   Houghton Mifflin.

A Final Word About Words

Verbs. When we read, we tend to look mostly at nouns — the names of people, places and things — that's where the information is. But as writers, the words we want to focus on are the verbs: that's where the action is.

One kind of verb you may want to take a second look at:

Forms of the verb "to be." There's nothing wrong with these verb forms. The problem is they are the most popular verb forms in the English language, and they've lost some of their power. If you've written five or six sentences in a row and all your verbs are linked with any of these six words — "am," "is," "are," "was," "were," "been" — see if you can replace a few of these constructions with other verbs or verb forms. A sentence such as "He is going to be here on Tuesday," for example, could be changed to "He arrives on Tuesday."

Adjectives. Because we live in an advertising age, we've learned not to pay attention to adjectives. We've learned to see through the illusion of advertising to the specific details underneath. The specific details about any subject — person, place, product, service or idea — are what grabs the strongest hold on our imaginations. Compare "The new computer has proven to be a cost-effective alternative to the old word processors" with "The RAM has cut our operating costs by 30%." Or "Management needs to be apprised of possibilities for entering international markets with new products" with "Twenty percent of the British clerical force lacks a computer-centered data base."

When you've finished the first draft of any writing, go back and circle adjectives you've used. After each adjective, ask yourself this question: "What do I mean by this word?" Take the first answer that comes to mind, cross out the adjective, and put what you mean in its place.

If, however, you think the adjective accurately captures your feel for the subject, leave the adjective; but in the next sentence, give a specific example of what you mean. To say your boss has bad manners doesn't stir your reader's imagination nearly as much as saying your boss makes you babysit for his daughter, clean his aquarium and take his dirty clothes to the laundry.

8

MECHANICS

"Nothing you write, if you hope to be good, will come out as you first hoped." — Lillian Hellman

Business professionals expect your writing to be correct. No matter how brilliant your ideas or provocative your analyses, mechanical mistakes will undermine your credibility.

What is "correct" or "incorrect," however, is not the province of any one person or school of thought. It belongs to the people who speak the language. They create the rules and, because language is like life, the rules are not always consistent. The rules, like people, sometimes change and sometimes contradict each other. What's true in one situation doesn't hold up in another. Or what was true one year no longer applies now. It used to be you couldn't split an infinitive or end a sentence with a preposition. Now you can. Many well-educated, accomplished writers begin their sentences with "And" or "But," and follow the singular "none" with a plural verb ("None of you are wrong"). Because language is constantly changing, it's conceivable that in the not too distant future it will be acceptable to not distinguish between "who" and "whom," substitute "like" for "as," and comma splice as many sentences as desired.

But what about today? How can you get a handle on what's acceptable in a business memo or letter and what isn't? How can you resolve the conflict between what is "correct" and what is "incorrect"?

Be Yourself. The closer you write to the way you speak, the more powerful, lively, engaging and "correct" your writing will be. You speak in simple, clear, easy to understand sentences. These sentences are easy to construct and punctuate. Compare the sentence below with what follows it:

> The Privacy Act of 1974 provides that each federal agency inform individuals, whom it asks to supply information, of the authority for the solicitation of the information and whether disclosure of such information is mandatory or voluntary; the principle purpose or purposes for which the information is to be used; the routine uses which may be made of the information; and the effects on the individual of not providing the information.

> The Privacy Act of 1974 says that each federal agency that asks you for information must tell you whether the law says you have to give it, what the agency wants the information for, and what will happen to you if you do not give it.

Both sentences say the same thing, but the first is much more difficult to read. And because it is written like the writer thinks a message like this should sound, the chances of a misinterpretation on the part of the reader are greatly increased. The second sentence, though also long, is easier to read and much easier to punctuate. The closer you can write to the way you speak, the more you cut down on your chances of making a mechanical mistake.

Assume a New Identity. After you've finished being yourself on paper, become a copyeditor. You want to see what you said, not what you wanted to say.

The best way to do this is to:

1. Sit back and relax.
2. Read your memo or letter several times through the same way your reader would.
3. Allow your mistakes to emerge naturally from the page.

If you find some mistakes still slipping through:

1. Put a blank piece of paper over all the lines of your memo or letter except the last.
2. Read the last line backwards.
3. Move the paper up one line and read backwards the second line from the last.
4. Do this for the entire memo or letter.

This will help you discover misspelled words and typographical errors. Then reverse the process. Start with the first line and work your way down through the memo or letter. You'll discover the times you write "their" for "there" or "too" for "to." If you come across a phrase or sentence that you're not sure is correct, read it out loud. Your ears will tell you. If the sentence sounds right, it probably is even if it doesn't conform to someone else's idea of what's right and wrong.

Nevertheless, we want to be correct. Consult your company's policy regarding business correspondence or one of the following guides on grammar and usage:

The Elements of Style. William Strunk, Jr. and E.B. White. The Macmillan Company.

Harbrace College Handbook. John C. Hodges and Mary E. Whitten. Harcourt Brace Jovanovich.

When Words Collide. Lauren Kessler and Duncan McDonald. Wadsworth Publishing Company.

9

SPELLING

*"It's a damn poor mind that can think of only one
way to spell a word."* — Andrew Jackson

If you're a poor speller, you'll probably always be a poor
speller. Spelling is not a sign of intelligence; it's a question of
brain function. Some people have it and some people don't —
the same way some people are more suited to math and others
are more suited to literature. Nevertheless, there are a few
things you can do to cut down on your spelling mistakes:

Stick to the Words You Say. Ninety percent of all good
writing consists of only a thousand words. These thousand
words are the same words we say every day. Studies show that
we know how to spell practically all of the words we say. In
fact, we don't say many words we don't know how to spell. If,
when you write, you only use words that you say, you're going
to cut down on your spelling mistakes. Following is a list of the

kinds of words we tend to say and the kind we tend to write. Notice how much more difficult to spell are the ones we tend to write:

Words We Say .... *Words We Write*

make easy .... facilitate
trouble .... inconvenience
about .... pertaining to
home .... residence
show .... reveal
later .... subsequent
enough .... sufficient
happen .... transpire
stop .... terminate

Pronounce Words Carefully. If you pronounce them correctly, you stand a good chance of spelling them correctly:

library   accidentally   surprise   February

Watch for Words That Sound Alike:

accept-except   altar-alter   passed-past
vain-vein   here-hear   it's-its

Watch for Words That Look Alike:

loose-lose   choose-chose   proceed-precede
quite-quit   moral-morale   personal-personnel

Look for Prefixes. Few people have trouble spelling the everyday words learned as children ("eye," "thought," "one") regardless of how difficult the spelling or the pronunciation. The words that cause the most spelling trouble are the ones we learned from reading. Many of these came from other languages, especially Latin, and most consist of three parts: a prefix, a base to which prefixes and suffixes are attached, and a suffix.

Spelling words with prefixes is difficult because we don't use the words very often, we don't recognize the prefix as a prefix, and the same prefix may be spelled in different ways for different words.

Fortunately, we know enough of these prefix-stem-suffix constructions that we don't have to be Latin scholars to understand them. Nevertheless, we can improve our spelling ability — and develop our vocabularies — by breaking words down into their parts. Say, for example, we know the meaning of the prefix "uni-": "one" or "single." And say we know the meaning of the word "uniform." Then we come across a word we might not know: "unilateral." Knowing the prefix gives us a clue in determining the meaning.

Guidelines for Prefixes

Although there are numerous inconsistencies in spelling words with prefixes, there are a few rules that hold true in most cases:

1. The spelling of the base or root of a word is never changed by the addition of a prefix.

- mis + spell = misspell
- trans + plant = transplant
- un + necessary = unnecessary
- a + rouse = arouse

2. Many prefixes also keep the same form, regardless of the base or root to which they are attached.

dis/appear	dis/appoint	dis/satisfied
for/bid	for/sake	for/swear

3. Some prefixes change their last letter to fit better with the words they are attached to.

ad/mit	ad/junct	aggression
en/grave	en/ter	empower

4. *Some prefixes* (and these are the most troublesome) *are similar in sound but are spelled differently.*

    - ante (meaning before); antedate, antecedent
    - anti (meaning against); anticlimax, antibody

    - inter (meaning between); interpret, interrupt
    - intra (meaning within); intramural, intravenous

Watch for Suffixes. If the root word ends with an "e," and the first letter of the ending you want to add begins with a vowel ("a," "e," "i," "o," "u," or "y"), drop the "e" before adding your ending:

> arrang(e)ing   com(e)ing   combin(e)ation

If your ending doesn't begin with a vowel, keep the "e."

> careful   entirely   placement

Two exceptions: If the root word ends with a vowel ("a," "e," "i," "o," "u," or "y") and the letter before the vowel is a "c" or a "g," keep the vowel if you're adding an ending that begins with an "a" or an "o."

> notice/able   change/able   manage/able

Notice How Other People Spell. Not just the words you have trouble with but new ones as well. Books, magazines, newspapers, even restaurant menus can help. Consider reading with a pen — underline the correct spelling of the words you have trouble with, list them on a piece of paper, and tape them to your bulletin board or the inside of your desk drawer. That way you don't have to look them up every time you want to use them.

Many words have two or more acceptable spellings. This is especially true of words that come from languages that do not use the Latin alphabet. "Usable," for example, can also be spelled "useable." The first spelling that appears in your dictionary is the most common. Unless your company suggests otherwise, use the most common spelling. Here is a short list of words that can be spelled more than one way.

sulfur/sulphur	combating/combatting
labeled/labelled	luster/lustre
theater/theatre	caliph/kalif

10

PUNCTUATION

"Those who write clearly have readers;
those who write obscurely have commentators."
— Albert Camus

Punctuation marks are like traffic signals. They direct readers where you want them to go. A period (.) means to come to a full stop, a semicolon (;) means to stop and proceed, a comma (,) means to slow down, and the absence of any punctuation means to keep going. Writers and readers, like drivers, move smoothly when they obey the signs. Look at the difference a comma makes in the following sentences:

> Let's talk turkey.
> Let's talk, turkey.

Although there are many rules governing punctuation, they don't solve all the punctuation problems. Decisions about whether or where to use a particular punctuation mark often involve questions of style and emphasis — issues that cannot always be reduced to a set of rules. Like style, punctuation is something of an art and, like art, can be developed through the use and practice of certain skills. Punctuation marks are the tools writers use to make their art more accessible to the reader.

In this book, punctuation problems are covered selectively, that is, with an emphasis on correcting the errors that appear most frequently in business writing.

The Comma

A Comma and a Conjunction Join Two Sentences:

- The report has been issued, and its recommendations have been accepted.

- The new photocopy machine will save us time, but we have to walk to another building to get to it.

A Comma Separates an Introduction From the Main Part of a Sentence:

- Because Dr. Jones will be lecturing in London this week, Wednesday's meeting has been cancelled.

- On the other hand, our profits were much higher than we expected.

A Comma Separates Information That Isn't Part of the Main Sentence:

- National Seminars, located in Kansas, offers a wide range of courses.

- The program, because it wasn't carefully thought out, was difficult to maintain.

A Comma Separates Elements in a Simple Series.

The flag is red, white and blue.

Notice the absence of the comma before the conjunction "and." Problems occur, however, in a complex sentence where the absence of the comma confuses the reader. For example:

Mary's areas of study are the Harlem Renaissance, Contemporary Women Writers and Feminist Literary Criticism.

Is Mary studying two or three areas? Therefore, the guideline is don't include the comma in a simple series; include the comma when leaving it out might cause confusion.

Commas Identify Quotations:

Mark Twain tells us, "There are two times in a man's life when he should not speculate: when he can't afford it and when he can."

"The business of America," said Calvin Coolidge, "is business."

"Lobbyists are the touts of protected industries," Winston Churchill told the press.

Commas Separate Words From Those They Are Sometimes Connected With:

Los Angeles, California, is the home of the Dodgers; Anaheim, California, is the home of the Angels. The way the people drive there, you are either one or the other.

There are, however, some exceptions to this rule: Sr., Jr., Ph.D., M.D., D.Ed., Inc., Ltd., and esq. — though you wouldn't be wrong if you left the comma in. Both of the following are correct:

- Andrew Rabinowitz, M.D. is giving the lecture.
- Andrew Rabinowitz, M.D., is giving the lecture.

The most important thing to remember is consistency. Establish which is your organization's preferred usage and be consistent.

When the title is part of a name, eliminate all the commas. You'd never write Earl, the Pearl, for example. "Earl the Pearl, Nate the Snake, and Deam the Dream were all Knicks."

The Comma Splice

The comma splice is two independent sentences joined incorrectly with a comma.

"Mary mailed the envelope, John received the letter."

To make the sentences correct, you could replace the comma with a semicolon:

"Mary mailed the envelope; John received the letter."

Another option is to separate the two independent thoughts into two sentences. Yet a third possibility is to use a comma and a coordinating conjunction.

"Mary mailed the envelope, and John received the letter."

To determine whether you want to separate your sentences with a period, a semicolon or a comma and a conjunction, read them out loud. Each solution will give your sentences a slightly different tone or meaning. By reading them out loud, you can also best determine the most effective structure. The most appropriate structure, however, will probably be your company's policy regarding comma splices.

The Colon

Use the Colon to Announce an Important Statement, a List of Items, or a Long Quotation.

Corporation: an ingenious device for obtaining individual profit without individual responsibility.

There are three kinds of salespeople: those who are winners and know they are winners, those who are losers and know they are losers and those who are winners but don't know it. The last are the most dangerous. They never give up trying.

Ron Luciano tells us: "When I started as an umpire, baseball was played by nine tough competitors on grass in graceful ballparks. By the time I retired, there were ten men on each side, the game was played indoors on plastic, and I had to spend half my time watching out for a man dressed in a chicken suit who kept trying to kiss me."

The Semicolon

When there were only the period and the comma, there were only two rules: if you want to make a long pause between two thoughts, put in a period; if you want to make a short pause, put in a comma. The semicolon was invented to create a longer pause than a comma and a shorter pause than a period. Since then it has become one of the most hated punctuation marks. Most writers don't use it.

The most common use for the semicolon today is to join two sentences. The semicolon enables the sentence to move a little more quickly than if a period separated the two sentences:

Promotion should not be more important than accomplishment; avoiding instability should not be more important than taking the risk.

The Dash

Because it speeds the reader along, the dash has virtually replaced the colon (:). Written with one space on either side, the dash looks as if it might be an arrow pointing your reader's way to an important part of the sentence. In this sense, it is an effective way to attract and direct the reader's attention:

> The business of government is to keep the government out of business — unless, of course, the business needs the government.

The dash can also serve the same function as parentheses. Parentheses offer high visibility, but they slow the reader down and look somewhat formal compared to dashes. Dashes give the impression of speech:

> "The money getters — those to whom we owe our academies, colleges and churches — are the real benefactors of our race."   — P.T. Barnum.

The dash can be used to show attribution, as in the quotation by P.T. Barnum, and it can also be used to insert information before concluding the sentence:

> The news of Edward R. Murrow's death — reportedly from cancer — was followed on CBS by a cigarette commercial.

The danger with dashes is that — because of their popularity — people tend to overuse them. There's nothing wrong with this — at least not yet — but too many dashes — as the sentences in this paragraph demonstrate — weaken the effect of the dash, slow the reader down, and can rob other punctuation marks of their meaning and use.

The Hyphen

Hyphens Join Two or More Words to Create a Single Unit.

Hyphens join two or more words, but the new word they form usually creates a meaning that is different from what the individual words mean by themselves. The most common example is the word "basketball." When the two words were first joined, they were linked by a hyphen: "basket-ball." But repeated use of the new compound made the word so familiar that the hyphen could be dropped. The same is true for "skyscraper," "briefcase" and "airport."

Though dozens of words have made the transition from hyphenated compounds to single words, hundreds of others have not. These words have either not received the common usage of a word such as "basketball," or the absence of the hyphen could cause confusion. A *dictionary* is the best source for determining which compounds have made the passage to one word and which have not. Nevertheless, there are some guidelines to follow when hyphenating words.

Guidelines for Hyphens

1. Hyphenate two or more words functioning as a single unit.

- his *never-say-die* attitude (adjective)
- his grip was a *bone-crusher* (noun)
- the muggers *pistol-whipped* him (verb)

Note that, unlike the dash, hyphens are not separated from the words they connect by a space on either side.

2. Hyphenate two-word numbers when they are written out.

Twenty-one days from now, she will be here.

3. Hyphenate words that are combined with the prefixes "ex-" and "self-."

The *ex-president* felt very *self-conscious.*

4. Hyphenate prefixes like "anti-," "pro-" and "pre-" when the first letter of the next word begins with a capital letter.

She was *anti-Establishment*, but she was also *pro-American.*

5. Hyphenate words when not to do so would cause confusion.

- *re-cover* (the chair) ....*recover* (the lost wallet)
- *re-sign* (the contract) ....*resign* (from office)

6. Hyphenate words that are suspended in a sentence.

He will take a two- to four-year leave of absence.

If this kind of construction looks odd to you or you're not sure if what you've written is correct, consider rewriting the sentence:

He will take a leave of absence for two to four years.

The Apostrophe

Use the Apostrophe to Form the Plural Case of a Noun.

1. Show possession with an 's for singular nouns and an s' for plural nouns.

singular nouns	plural nouns
manager's	managers'
president's	presidents'
worker's	workers'

2. **Show possession with nouns that form their plural in ways other than by adding an "s" by adding 's to the plural of the noun.**

singular nouns	*plural nouns*
man's	men's
woman's	women's
child's	children's

3. **Show possession of singular nouns ending in "s" by adding an apostrophe or by adding an 's.**

singular nouns	*plural nouns*
• *boss's car*	• *dress's button*
• *boss' signature*	• *dress' seam*

4. **Another way to show possession of singular nouns ending in "s," although less widely acceptable, is by adding an apostrophe.**

   - waitress' sandwich
   - press' notebook
   - actress' skit

5. **To show possession of plural nouns ending in "s," add an apostrophe to the end of the word.**

   - boys' fame
   - writers' network
   - executives' club
   - bosses' decision

6. **To form the possessive of pairs of nouns, add 's to the second noun in instances of joint possession:**

   - John and Mary's office
   - the brother and sister's car
   - the men and women's pool

7. Add 's to each member of the pair in instances of individual possession:

- John's and Mary's computers
- the brother's and sister's cars
- the men's and women's pools

8. To show possession for group nouns or compound nouns, add 's to the end of the unit:

group nouns	compound nouns
association's	editor-in-chief's
team's	someone else's
committee's	president-elect's

9. To show possession for compounds that form their plural by adding "s" to the first word, add 's to the end of the unit.

- editors-in-chief's
- sons-in-law's
- writers in residence's

10. Avoid confusion when adding an apostrophe to some plural words.

- Jackson received two Es on his scorecard.
- He now stirs drinks for the Oakland As.

What are the "do's" and "don'ts" here? Ask yourself, what helps my reader best? Obviously "do's" is better than "dos"; "don'ts" is better than "donts"; "A's" is more effective than "As"; and "Es" is understandable left as is or written "E's."

The Ellipsis

The Ellipsis (three spaced periods) indicates that a series of words have been omitted from a direct quotation:

The manager said, "Our customers . . . are unhappy."

To show the deletion of whole sentences, add another period to the ellipsis:

The results are irrelevant . . . . A similar document could be produced to conclude the exact opposite.

The correct way to write an ellipsis is with one space on either side.

Quotation Marks

Quotation marks can be used to emphasize a word or cite an example, but they have two main functions:

1. To Show What Someone Said.

Albert Camus wrote, "The society of money and exploitation has never been charged, so far as I know, with assuring the triumph of freedom and justice."

On the other hand, Woodrow Wilson tells us, "Every great man of business has got somewhere a touch of the idealist in him."

2. To Identify the Title of a Short Story, Poem, Article, Song, Chapter in a Book, One-Act Play or any Other Short Piece of Writing. Titles of longer works — books, plays, movies, newspapers and magazines — are commonly italicized or underlined.

"Raindrops Keep Falling on My Head" set just the
right mood for William Goldman's *Butch Cassidy
and the Sundance Kid.*

Quotation Marks and Other Punctuation

The major problem with quotation marks comes when you
mix them with periods, commas and question marks. This poses
no problems for a sentence such as:

Yogi Berra said, "If people don't want to come out
to the ballpark, nobody's going to stop them."

But what if the speaker asks a question about the words in
the quotation? Then the question mark should go outside the
quotation:

Did Yogi really say, "Nobody's going to stop them"?

Periods and commas go inside the quotation marks; colons
and semicolons go outside. Question marks may go inside or
outside depending on who is doing the talking.

Did Yogi say, "Nobody is going to stop them"?
She asked, "What did Yogi say?"

Exclamations!

Don't use too many of them! Save them for when they
count! Otherwise, like the boy who cried wolf, your exclamations won't be taken seriously!!!

11

SYNTAX

"All the fun's in how you say a thing."
— Robert Frost

Syntax is the way we arrange our words when we write or speak. If you're a native speaker of English, you know all you need to know about how to structure a sentence. You've been structuring sentences all your life. As long as you write as close as possible to the way you speak, you will almost always arrange your words in simple, clear, easy-to-understand sentences.

There are a few times, however, when help is needed. No one has difficulty with all of the syntax problems discussed in this chapter, but most people have trouble with one or two of them. After you've learned to correct the problems that appear most frequently in your writing, keep a special lookout for them when proofreading. These are the mistakes that business writers tend to make over and over again.

Subject-Verb Agreement

Singular subjects take singular verbs ("He goes to the office"), and plural subjects require plural verbs ("They go to the office"). But sometimes we place our verbs so far away from our subjects that we match our verbs with some other word in the sentence. This other word almost always is located between the subject and the verb. For example, we can express this thought with little difficulty:

The *projections seem* to be holding up.

"Seem" agrees in number with "projections." Problems occur, however, when we start placing words between "projections" and "seem." For example:

The *projections*, despite strong evidence, *seems* to be holding up.

Because "evidence," was the last word to come into my mind before writing the verb "seems," I incorrectly matched "seems" with "evidence" rather than with "projections," the word "seem" should refer to.

The most irritating thing about agreement problems is that we know better. Not only do we know that subjects and verbs have to match, we know how to match them. Unfortunately, we get distracted by the other words in the sentence.

Even when we're not distracted by other words in the sentence, there are certain situations that cause many people trouble:

Singular nouns joined by "and" require a plural verb because there are now two subjects in the sentence:

John *and* Mary arrive on time.

The few exceptions to this rule are almost all the expressions of a particular culture or dialect:

• Rock 'n roll is here to stay.
• Peanut butter and jelly is on its way.

In these cases, as in most others, your ear is the best judge for determining the most effective syntax.

Nouns joined by "or" or "nor" use singular verbs if all the nouns are singular:

Either John or Mary *has* to give in.

Nouns joined by "or" or "nor" use plural verbs if all the nouns are plural:

Neither the men nor the women *want* to submit.

When one noun is singular and the other noun is plural, the verb agrees in number with the closest noun.

Neither John nor the women *want* to continue.

Noun-Pronoun Agreement

Pronouns, which are substitutes for nouns, have two things in common with nouns: number (singular or plural) and gender (masculine, feminine or neuter). What they don't have in common is person. All nouns are third person, but some pronouns are first person ("I," "we"), some are second person ("you"), and some are third person ("he," "she," "it," "they," "one," "some," "none," "all," "everybody," "somebody").

A pronoun in any sentence must agree with the noun it refers to in person, number and gender.

Person: "The president assigned some *sales people* to the project, but she knew *it* wouldn't help." The neuter pronoun "it" cannot refer to "people." The correct pronoun is "they."

Number: "The *testing* of the new security devices should be nearing *their* final stage." The plural pronoun "their" cannot refer to the singular noun "testing." The correct pronoun is "its."

Gender: "The old *car* did *her* best, but the hill was too much." The feminine pronoun "her" should not be linked with a neuter noun. The correct pronoun is "its."

Mismatching nouns and pronouns in person and gender is not a common error; mismatching nouns and pronouns in number is. Much of the trouble involving number has to do with words such as "everyone," "everybody," "all," "none," "some" and "each."

Everyone, everybody, anybody and anyone take singular verbs and should be referred to with singular pronouns:

"*Anybody* who wants to enter has to pay *her* fee by Friday."

All and *some* are singular or plural depending on the context they appear in. Both words are often followed by "of." If what comes after the "of " is a mass or bulk of something, the pronoun is singular:

Some of the material lost its color.

If what comes after the "of " refers to a number of things or persons, the pronoun is plural:

Some of the agents lost their notebooks.

Traditionally, *none* is singular or plural depending on the context, but the distinction of singular or plural within certain contexts is so subtle that either a singular or a plural pronoun would be correct:

None of the sales people *was* willing to submit *his* or *her* report.

Also correct is:

None of the sales people *were* willing to submit *their* reports.

On the other hand, the singular forms *was* and *his* would be hard to justify in this sentence:

None of the salespeople *were* as good as *their* managers.

Each is always singular:

Each renewed her dedication to increased sales.

Unless, of course, "each" refers to a group whose members are both male and female. In this case, the plural pronoun "they" is acceptable, but the more grammatically appropriate sentence would be:

The sales people renewed their dedication to increased sales.

Modifiers

A modifier is a word that changes or in some way alters the meaning of another word. For this reason, modifiers should be placed as close as possible to the words they modify. To put them somewhere else can cause readers to understand something different than intended.

Old and in disrepair, I bought the building cheap.

The building may be in better shape than the buyer.

The president explained why coffee breaks were detrimental to business on Monday.

The rest of the week coffee breaks were okay.

Read your sentences out loud. Your ear is a great aid in revealing the misplacement of modifying words and phrases.

Fragments

When we were in grammar school, we were taught that a sentence is a complete thought. It had a subject and a verb. We were also taught that a fragment was an incomplete thought. It lacked a subject or a verb and, therefore, was unacceptable. We pointed out that many of the writers we were asked to read wrote in fragments. Were they wrong? We were told these writers had a poetic license. When we were famous writers, we could write in fragments too. Until then, we would write in complete sentences.

The idea stuck with us and, as a result, many writers feel uncomfortable when they see a sentence fragment in print. What we have to realize is that fluent speakers of English write and converse in fragments all the time. They do this because each is capable of supplying the missing words.

The problem, then, is not fragments but in how they are used. When you use a fragment, make sure you have a specific purpose or effect in mind. Make sure your fragment communicates clearly what you want to say to your reader.

> Although the report reached his desk in time . . .

This is an ineffective fragment. There are too many missing words for the reader to supply.

> The company was in a nosedive. Until November.
> That's when Mike Flannagan took over.

"Until November" is an effective fragment; it emphasizes the date on which the company began its rebound.

> I need your help. Now!

Like "Until November," "Now!" has neither a subject nor a predicate, but the powerful effect of the word could not have been achieved — or achieved as well — in a complete sentence.

The points to be made by these examples are:

1. Fragments are an ordinary, everyday part of the English language. In this sense, they are grammatically correct.

2. Fragments, when used properly, are not only an effective means of communication, they are stylistically desirable.

Run-on Sentences

Sentences must be separated by a period, a semicolon or a conjunction such as "and" or "but." A run-on sentence joins two sentences without placing any punctuation or conjunction between them. This sentence joins two complete thoughts without any punctuation mark:

> Wallace Stevens was a poet he was also the president of an insurance company.

This sentence joins two complete thoughts with a traditionally improper punctuation mark: the comma between poet and he. The name for this error is "comma splice."

> Wallace Stevens was a poet, he was also the president of an insurance company.

To punctuate this sentence correctly in business writing, there are three possibilities:

1. Wallace Stevens was a poet. He was also the president of an insurance company.
    or
2. Wallace Stevens was a poet; he was also the president of an insurance company.
    or
3. Wallace Stevens was a poet, but he was also the president of an insurance company.

Parallel Construction

Parallelism means using the same grammatical structure for all the items in a sentence that have the same function. Parallelism not only holds sentences together, it adds emphasis, provides flow, expresses thoughts more clearly, makes reading more pleasurable, takes up less space and makes what we say easy to remember. This is why so many famous quotations are in parallel forms:

- I came, I saw, I conquered.
- A penny saved is a penny earned.
- Do unto others as you would have them do unto you.

Faulty parallelism occurs when the second or successive items in a parallel series do not fit the pattern established by the first item. For example,

Eating is time-consuming, expensive, and it makes you fat.

The proper construction for this sentence should be:

Eating is time-consuming, expensive and fattening.

Correct faulty parallelism by putting all the related ideas into the same grammatical form.

Tense

Most verbs are written in the present, past or future tense. Sometimes, however, writing requires a shift from one tense to another. If, for example, we are contrasting past action with present action, or demanding action in the future based on what is taking place in the present, we need to shift tenses. Errors occur when we don't change the tense of the verb to fit the action we are expressing. Here's an example:

I *asked* the manager where I *could get* a copy of the report, and he *tells* me I *will have to see* the president.

This sentence unnecessarily shifts from the past to the present tense with the word "tells." The logical way to write this sentence is:

I *asked* the manager where I *could get* a copy of the report, and he *told* me I *would have to see* the president.

Generally speaking, if you begin writing in one tense, stay in that tense. If you have to change, consider beginning a new paragraph every time you shift tenses. A new paragraph alerts the reader that a change may be coming, and a new paragraph helps your reader understand your message more clearly.

Transitions

Proper transition is necessary for coherence. There should be transitions between paragraphs, between sentences, and even between words in long sentences. The best transitional device is a logical presentation of your ideas; there simply is no substitute for getting ideas into their proper order in the first place and avoiding interruptions or irrelevant details later.

Transitional words relate what we have said to what we are going to say. Readers rely heavily on transitional words to establish the logic of sentences and groups of sentences. Misuse of transitional words changes the meaning of the message. Consider the following sentence:

While she was only a child, Mary could solve problems in algebra.

Does this mean that Mary is a child or that she was a child? If Mary is no longer a child, a more effective transition would be "when"; if Mary is a child, "although" would be a less confusing choice than "while."

- When she was only a child, Mary could solve problems in algebra.

- Although she was only a child, Mary could solve problems in algebra.

The careless use of "and" or "but" also detracts from clarity:

- I bought a typewriter, and Dean bought a computer.

- I bought a typewriter, but Dean bought a computer.

"And" means "in addition to"; "but" implies some kind of contrast or something contrary to what was expected. Choose the transition that conveys the exact meaning you intend.

If the reader doesn't understand what you are saying, no amount of tinkering to achieve emphasis or variety can salvage the writing. Have something to say and say it in an organized way. If a piece of writing has no focus, even an effective transition will not give it one.

Capitalization

Capitalization is determined by convention. Unless you have a specific reason for not doing so, obey the conventions. Here are some guidelines that can help:

1. Capitalize the first word of every sentence.
2. Capitalize the proper names of people, places and things: *Bob, New York, the White House.*
3. Capitalize words derived from proper names: *American, Edwardian.*
4. Capitalize the days of the week: *Monday, Tuesday.*
5. Capitalize the months of the year: *January, May.*
6. Capitalize names of holidays: *Christmas, Labor Day.*
7. Capitalize historical documents: *Declaration of Independence.*
8. Capitalize historical events and ages: *Reformation.*
9. Capitalize common names with place names: *Mississippi River, Fifth Avenue.*
10. Capitalize the main words in titles: *Moby Dick, New York Times.*
11. Capitalize titles of offices when used directly before a name: *Senator Kennedy, President Wilson.*

12. Capitalize the words "president" and "governor" without a name if they refer to the *President of the United States* or the *Governor of* a state.
13. Capitalize "vice" when used in front of a name: *Vice-President Quayle.*
14. Capitalize the names of family members when used with a name: *Uncle Dick, Grandma Moses.*

Abbreviations

Abbreviations are seldom used in formal writing. Nevertheless, here are some guidelines:

1. *Omit the period after letters of an organization:* CCNY (City College of New York), ROTC (Reserve Officers Training Corps), HEW (Health, Education and Welfare).

2. *Not all abbreviations are written the same way:* MPH (miles per hour) can be written mph, Mph, m.p.h. If your company doesn't have a specific preference, choose the way you like best. Make sure, however, that you are consistent throughout any memo or letter you write.

Some Common Abbreviations

a.m.	*ante meridiem*, before noon
p.m.	*post meridiem*, after noon
e.g.	*exempli gratia*, for example
i.e.	*id est*, that is
ibid.	*ibidem*, in the same place
viz.	*videlicet*, namely
etc.	*et cetera*, and so forth

Acronyms

An acronym is a special kind of abbreviation. It is formed by the first letter or letters of each word in a name or phrase. CIA, for example, is an acronym for Central Intelligence

Agency, and sonar is an acronym for sound navigation ranging. Some acronyms are pronounced as if they were independent words. The acronym for North Atlantic Treaty Organization, for example, is pronounced as the word "NATO"; we don't say "N-A-T-O."

The use of acronyms has increased greatly in the twentieth century, but not everyone knows every acronym. Unless the acronym is used in everyday speech ("DNA" instead of "deoxyribonucleic acid"), spell out the complete word or title on first reference and place the acronym immediately afterwards in a set of parentheses. Then use the acronym for all future references.

> Jose Rodriguez began working for Minnesota Mining and Manufacturing (3M) in 1964. Today he is vice-president of 3M Research and Development.

Numerals

Numbers in writing are governed by convention. Here are the standard guidelines, though your company's or subject field's policies may vary:

1. *Spell-out numbers one through nine:*

    • There were four people at the meeting.

2. *Use the number for numerals above 10 unless the word for that number is shorter or easier to read than the number itself:*

    • There were 14 people at the meeting.
    • He sold the company for a million dollars.

3. *Do not begin a sentence with an arabic numeral:*

    • 600 employees work for Acme, Inc.

This sentence should be written:

- Six hundred employees work for Acme, Inc.

or

- A total of 600 employees work for Acme, Inc.

4. Spell out numbers under 101 when they are used as adjectives.

- In the early twentieth century, there were fewer four-year colleges.

5. Do not spell out dates or numbers that are part of a series:

- September 19, 1961.
- Chapter II

6. Use arabic numbers with a.m. and p.m. Use o'clock and morning or afternoon when the number is in script.

- The meeting went to 7 p.m.
- The meeting went to seven in the evening.

or

- The meeting went to seven o'clock in the evening.

12

WRITING FOR BUSINESS

"Every style that is not boring is a good one."
— Voltaire

Make Business Writing Conversational

Most of what we find dull in business correspondence is not *what* we say but *how* we say it. Just because we work for an institution is no reason why we have to sound like one. The most effective business correspondence, like the best writing anywhere, is short, clear and personal. Phrases such as "prioritized evaluative procedures" and "modified departmental agenda" only make readers work harder to understand the message. This leads to frustration and resentment. Those who come across as people make the best impressions, win the most customers and earn the most money. They even make friends.

Before writing any memo or letter, ask yourself this important question: *Is this necessary?* One of the secrets to writing effective memos and letters is limiting yourself to correspondence that counts. Most memos and letters are too long, sent to too many people, and written by people who write too many of them. They also take time and energy to write. Telephoning in many cases is faster, more personal and more effective. If there are any questions, you can answer them right away. Correspondence, on the other hand, can't adjust to a reader's reaction the way a speaker adjusts to a listener's. Nor can you change what you've written once you've sent it out.

The advantage of memos and letters is that they force us to articulate our thoughts. Readers can read them again if they're not sure about something. They can show them to others to help eliminate hearsay and rumors.

Memos and letters also have a way of encouraging others to act. People may be able to avoid running into us or forget what we said on the phone, but they have a harder time ignoring something that's staring up at them from the desk. They know the only way to get rid of that memo or letter is to act on it.

For this reason, written correspondence saves time. It's not as easy as talking on the phone, but it enables us to reach more people simultaneously and, if it is well written, we won't have to repeat ourselves.

Finally, written correspondence makes for good public relations. It gets our name seen, makes sure we get credit for our ideas, proves our ability to express ourselves, and frees us to complete other tasks.

Memos and Letters

No one has to work long in the business world to discover that writing is *the* universal currency for documenting what gets done and for formally expressing ideas. Every business person is by definition also a writer.

To write the most effective memos and letters:

1. Determine what you want to say and to whom you are saying it.

What

Don't be afraid to discuss your ideas with colleagues. Discussion not only helps you clarify what you want to say and how you want to say it, it also helps generate new ideas.

Whom

- What are my audience's needs?

- How much of what I want to say is relevant?

- Does what I have to say make a significant contribution to the reader's work?

- What's the best tone or approach to use for this particular reader or audience?

- What specific examples would best help my reader understand my message faster and respond more effectively?

2. Construct an Outline of What You Want to Say.

- Collect and review any relevant literature or previous documentation that has to do with your subject.

- Arrange your ideas in a clear, logical order.

- Get feedback from a colleague on the information you've selected as most important and how effectively you've ordered this information in your outline.

3. Write.

Sections of any memo or letter do not necessarily have to be written in sequence. Consider starting with the easiest sections; then, once you're warmed up, go into the more difficult parts.

Don't be a prisoner of your outline. Explore your thoughts. See where they might lead. Experiment with how different words and phrases sound.

Don't be afraid to cut a section and start over. Sometimes, our words just won't bend to the thoughts we have in mind. Back off and try a new approach.

4. Revise.

Again, don't be afraid to consult with a colleague. Ask yourself and your colleague these specific questions:

- *Is it short, clear and personal?* In a study of 800 letters, written by the top chief executive officers in the United States, all 800 letters were short, clear and personal. All the participants claimed they didn't get to be CEOs by writing letters the way other people told them business letters should sound. Each found out through his or her own experiences that the most effective letters were *short*, *clear* and *personal* and, by the time they became CEOs, they never once sent out a letter that didn't contain these three basic principles of good writing.

Questions to Help Assess the Effectiveness of Your Business Writing:

1. *Are my ideas arranged effectively?* In some cases, a chronological order is called for; in others, a step-by-step process. If you have a choice in determining your letter's order, consider this: people remember best what they read first; they remember second best what they read last.

2. *Does my opening sentence grab the reader's attention?* Consider writing it last. Once you have what you want to say on paper, go back and write an opening sentence that is short, clear, simple, easy to understand, grabs the reader's attention and makes the reader want to keep reading.

Writing the opening sentence last is much faster, easier and more effective than trying to come up with a sentence that covers what you're trying to say before you've even said it.

3. *Is my concluding sentence effective?* Second in importance only to the opening sentence, the concluding sentence is a good opportunity to induce some action on the part of the reader. Consider these concluding sentences:

- As soon as we hear from you, we will . . .
- Please call us if you . . .
- Will you please let us know if . . .
- Will you please handle this promptly?
- Can you arrange to . . .
- What is your opinion of . . .
- I'll call you next Thursday to see . . .

4. *Would any headings, lists, tables or graphs help clarify my meaning?* Concrete language and personal details are two ways of being specific, but nothing helps the images these words create in our minds as much as a good heading, list, table or graph.

The headings that punctuate this book offer good examples of how headings work. Open to any page. Notice how, before you begin to read a word on that page, your eyes are drawn to the heading?

Lists serve the same function as headings. They draw the reader's eyes onto the page and can suggest that there are a finite number of points to consider.

Consider, however, presenting your lists with bullets instead of the traditional number or letter sequence. Bullets can indicate that no item in the list is more important than any other and that there is no step-by-step process to follow. Numbered or lettered lists can indicate a step-by-step process or show items in order of importance. They may also be used to indicate a finite number of points.

If each of the items in your list is a complete thought, end each item with a period, or end the last item with a period and all the previous items listed with a semicolon or a comma. If the items are just words or short phrases, no punctuation is necessary.

For the best examples of tables and graphs, consider any issue of *USA TODAY*. Each issue includes first-rate examples of how tables and graphs can be attractively and effectively presented.

- ***Is it correct?*** Not just the information but the spelling of the reader's name. You'd be surprised at the difference a correctly spelled name makes in a reader's attitude toward you and your subject.

- ***Is my name legible?*** Your signature is the most personal part of any letter. Sign it with a pen you enjoy using, and make it legible.

- ***Is the postscript handwritten?*** Handwritten postscripts are often read before and then again after the letter is read. Be careful, however, that what you put in a postscript isn't so important as to make you look forgetful or careless.

- ***Have I correctly addressed my reader?*** People don't usually get upset if you don't address them by their proper salutation, but they notice and appreciate it when you do. Here are some common titles, addresses and proper salutations:

Title	Address on Envelope	Salutation in Letter
1. Admiral	Adm. (name), USN	Dear Admiral (name)
2. Ambassador	The Honorable (name)	Dear Mr./Ms. Ambassador
3. Archbishop	Most Rev. (name)	Dear Archbishop (name)
4. Archdeacon	The Venerable (name)	Venerable Sir or Madam
5. Attorney General	Hon. (name)	Dear Mr./Ms. (name)
6. Attorney	Mr./Ms. (name)	Dear Mr./Ms. (name)
7. Bishop (Catholic)	Most Rev. (name)	Dear Bishop (name)
8. Bishop (other)	Right Rev. (name)	Dear Bishop (name)
9. Colonel	Col.(name), USA, USAF, USMC	Dear Col. (name)
10. Commodore	Com. (name), USCG, USN	Dear Commodore (name)
11. Congressman	The Honorable (name)	Dear Mr./Ms. (name)
12. Consul	The (country) Consul	Dear Mr./Ms. (name)
13. Dean (church)	The Very Rev.	Very Rev. Sir or Madam
14. Dean (college)	Dean (name)	Dear Dean (name)
15. General	Gen. (name)	Dear Gen. (name)
16. Governor	The Honorable (name)	Dear Governor (name)
17. Judge	The Honorable (name)	Dear Judge (name)
18. Mayor	The Honorable (name)	Dear Mayor (name)
19. Minister (consul)	Hon. (name)	Dear Mr./Ms. (name)
20. Minister (clergy)	The Rev (name)	Dear Mr./Ms. (name)
21. Monsignor	The Right Rev. (name)	Dear Monsignor (name)
22. The Pope	His Holiness, Pope (name)	Your Holiness
23. Postmaster General	Hon. (name)	Dear Mr./Ms.
24. President (college)	Pres. (name, Ph.D.)	Dear Dr.
25. President (USA)	The President	Dear Mr./Ms. President
26. Priest	The Rev. (name)	Dear Father (name)
27. Principal	Dr./Mr./Mrs. (name)	Dear Dr./Mr./Mrs. (name)
28. Professor	Prof./ Dr. (name)	Dear Prof./Dr.
29. Rabbi	Rabbi (name)	Dear Rabbi (name)
30. Rector	The Very Rev. (name)	Dear Father (name)
31. Senator (USA)	The Hon. (name)	Dear Senator (name)
32. Sister	Sister (name)	Dear Sister (name)
33. Vice-President (USA)	The Hon. (name)	Dear Mr./Ms. Vice-President

Reports and Proposals

There are many kinds of reports and proposals, but most have one thing in common: to help someone make a decision. Before writing any report or proposal, ask the right questions. The more narrow your focus, the less abstract and difficult your job will be.

- What's the purpose of this report or proposal?
- Who's going to read it?
- What needs to be determined?
- Where specifically is the trouble located?
- When did the problem start?
- Have any attempts been made to correct it?
- What are the causes of the problem?
- What keeps the problem from being solved?

To write the proposal, follow the same steps detailed in the memos and letters section of this book. Then, after you've finished writing your report or proposal, ask yourself these four questions:

1. Have I provided the reader with all the necessary documentation?

2. Are my findings presented clearly at the beginning and end of the report or proposal?

3. Have I answered any questions that may come to the reader's mind?

4. Have I anticipated any objections?

Once you've written your report or proposal, plug what you've written into this or a similar format:

The Title Page. The title page should include the company's name, your name and the date on which the report or proposal is submitted. The title of the report or proposal should be written in capital letters. Follow company policy or your own judgment for titles of individual chapters, charts and graphs.

Titles and subheads written in all capital letters are usually difficult to read; so use sparingly sentences in which every word is capitalized. An effective way to set subheads apart from the main body of any report or proposal is to capitalize only the first letter of each major word. Articles and prepositions such as the following should be written in lower case:

a	at	for	on	the
an	but	if	or	to
as	by	in		

The Table of Contents. Though not always necessary, it can be helpful in lengthy reports or proposals, or ones that contain many subsections.

The Summary or Abstract. This is a one-page condensation that states explicitly your conclusions and recommendations.

The Introduction. Include a statement about the purpose of your report or proposal and your view of the problem or situation. Also include your conclusions and recommendations, but don't write them in the same way they appeared in the abstract. Consider including: the limitations of your report or proposal, the methods used to gather the information and any definitions of unfamiliar terms.

The Discussion. The main body of your report or proposal should: state your case, substantiate your points with specific details, and allow your reader to see the thought processes that led you to your conclusions and recommendations.

The Conclusion. Discuss in the conclusion: the relevance of your findings and any patterns or trends you discovered in your study that will help the reader with his or her decision about the subject of the report or proposal.

The Recommendation. Tell the reader how to put your conclusion into action.

The Bibliography. The bibliography lists the books and articles referred to in the report or proposal. Bibliography entries are usually arranged in alphabetical order by the author's last name:

Booth, Wayne C. *The Rhetoric of Fiction.* Chicago, IL: University of Chicago Press, 1961.
Frye, Northrop. *Anatomy of Criticism: Four Essays.* Princeton, NJ: Princeton University Press, 1957.

If the author isn't known, use the first word of the title or article. If the title begins with "A" or "The," use the second word.

Two or more books by the same author should appear in the bibliography as:

Frye, Northrop. *Anatomy of Criticism: Four Essays.* Princeton, NJ: Princeton University Press, 1957.
        The Critical Path: An Essay on the Social Context of Literary Criticism. Bloomington, IN: Indiana University Press, 1971.

Articles and stories are written as:

Levin, Yu. D. "Tolstoy, Shakespeare, and Russian Writers of the 1860's." *Oxford Slavonic Papers*, January 1985, pp. 15-23.

If the article or story appears within a chapter of a book, write:

Wright, Richard. "Bright and Morning Star." In *Short Stories: A Critical Anthology.* Ed. Ensaf Thune and Ruth Prigozy. New York, NY: Macmillan, 1973.

Cassette tapes are written the same way as books:

Andersen, Richard. *Powerful Business Writing Skills.*
Shawnee   Mission, KS: National Press Publications, Inc.,
1987.

Sections within a cassette tape are written the same way as articles:

Andersen, Richard. "How to Write a Complaint Letter,"
   Powerful Business Writing Skills. Shawnee Mission, KS:
   National Press Publications, 1987.

The Appendix. This section presents any data needed to support or expand upon the points made in the main body of your report or proposal.

The Index. Necessary only in lengthy or complicated cases, the index is a detailed table of contents. It lists in alphabetical order almost every subject discussed in your report or proposal.

13

SOME MATTERS OF FORM

"Foolish consistency is the hobgoblin of little minds."
— Ralph Waldo Emerson

Equations. Don't try to record them on a typewriter or computer that isn't equipped with the necessary characters. Leave space for any equations you need and write them out in longhand later. If your document is to be printed, your equations will be typeset or penned in neatly by hand.

To make your equations clear, consider positioning them on a separate line in the text. Introduce equations as you would any words that form a part of a sentence:

The current in the wire is calculated by using Ohm's law:

$$E = IR$$

Academic Degrees. Professors holding the Ph.D. degree are commonly addressed as "Professor" or "Dr." Occasionally, the title is left out and "Ph.D." follows the name. The important thing is to choose one form or the other; don't combine them. "Prof. Bernard Bell, Ph.D." is redundant. If the holder of the Ph.D. is not affiliated with a college or university, use "Dr."

Complimentary Close. Complimentary closes should be followed by commas and only the first word needs to be capitalized:

- Sincerely,
- Sincerely yours,
- Cordially,
- With best regards,
- Yours truly,

Corrections and Insertions. Avoid these as much as possible; make your memo, letter, report or proposal look as good as it can. If you *have* to make a correction or insert a word or phrase, do it in type or ink directly above the line involved. Don't use the margins or write below the line.

Ragged or Justified Margins. Justified looks better on the page, but ragged is easier to read.

Dates. Do not abbreviate dates in a formal letter, report or proposal. Sept. 19th, 1989 and 9/19/89 are not acceptable; 19 September 1989 and September 19, 1989 are.

Endnotes and Footnotes. Endnotes appear at the end of a report or proposal; footnotes appear at the bottom of a page in a report or proposal. Both refer to something on the page which cites them. Both list their works the same way a bibliography does except for five things:

1. The first line of an endnote or footnote is indented.
2. The author's first name precedes his or her last.
3. There is not a period after the title of the work.
4. The section containing information about the publisher is placed in parentheses.
5. The pages from which the quotation is taken or the reference is made are listed.

Footnote:

> Robert Scholes. *The Nature of Narrative*
> (New York: Oxford University Press, 1966), pp.3-5.

Bibliography:

> Scholes, Robert. *The Nature of Narrative.*
> New York, NY: Oxford University Press, 1966.

Margins. Keep the same width for the right-hand and left-hand margins.

Pagination. Number pages consecutively in the upper right-hand corner or center them at the bottom of each page. Do not punctuate them by adding periods. Although the title page and the first page of the text are not numbered, the pages are still counted. The bibliography and index pages, on the other hand, are numbered.

Permissions. Although holders of a copyright may legally charge a fee for the reproduction of copyrighted material, United States copyright law states that a "fair use" of a copyrighted work for the purposes of "criticism, comment, news reporting, teaching, scholarship or research" is not an infringement of copyright. In other words, if you're not planning to publish your report or proposal or make any money from it, you don't have to seek permission from an author to quote from his or her work.

Salutations. "Dear Mr. Jones" and "Dear Ms. Smith" are most commonly recommended; "Dear Sir:" and "Gentlemen:" are not.

If you don't know the name of the person you're writing to, write "Dear Sir or Madam:" If you know the name but don't know if the reader is a man or a woman, leave out the salutation, replace it with a subject heading, or write "Dear (the person's name)." Use "Mrs." only if your reader indicates that she prefers "Mrs." to "Ms." She can indicate this preference by typing "Mrs." along with her full name printed under her signature.

Spacing. Anything longer than a letter should be double-spaced throughout, including quotations and notes.

Syllabication. When a word must be divided at the end of a line, consult a dictionary if you are not absolutely sure where to divide the word.

Typing and Paper. Clean type is essential. Avoid script or fancy print. Type on only one side of 8 1/2" by 11" good quality paper. Do not submit anything on "erasable" paper as it smudges easily and looks cheap.

A Final Word About Form

Unlike the rules of spelling, policies regarding form change from company to company and from year to year. If you're not sure what to do and there's no office grammarian around to ask, rely on your common sense. Do what you think works best. Then, once you've made your decision, stick to it. Your consistency will often lead others not to question — they'll assume you must be right — or they'll wonder if they are wrong. So many people have consistently written "alright" instead of "all right" that the new edition of *Webster's Dictionary* lists both spellings as acceptable. However, the preferred spelling is always listed first.

14
A FINAL CHECKLIST

"If any person wishes to write in a clear style,
let him first be clear in his thoughts."
— Goethe

Before sending out anything — memo, letter, report or proposal
— ask yourself these questions:

1. What's the purpose?

2. Have I said what I'm trying to say?

3. Does the message look good on the page?

4. Is it mechanically correct or at least consistent?

5. Have I checked any spellings, divided words, capitalizations, abbreviations and punctuations I'm not sure of?

6. Have I varied the length of the paragraphs and sentences to help keep the reader awake?

7. Are my ideas simply stated and presented in a clear, logical order?

8. Have I limited myself to one idea to each paragraph?

9. Is the letter as short as I can get it?

10. Are there any unnecessary words I can eliminate?

11. Have I chosen the best words to say what I want to say?

12. Is what I've written "reader-centered" as opposed to "author-centered"?

13. Have I tried to turn my negatives into positives?

14. Have I maintained my respect for the reader?

15. Have I eliminated all cliches, jargon, buzz words and bureaucratic phrases?

16. Have I written in my natural tone of voice?

17. Does the closing leave the reader with the main idea and inspire him or her to act?

Bibliography

Andersen, Richard. *Writing That Works: A Practical Guide for Business and Creative People.* New York, NY: McGraw-Hill, 1989.

Cypert, Samuel A. *Writing Effective Business Letters, Memos, Proposals and Reports.* Chicago, IL: Contemporary Books, 1984.

Elbow, Peter. *Writing Without Teachers.* New York, NY: Oxford University Press, 1973.

Ewing David. E. *Writing for Results in Business, Government, the Sciences and the Professions.* New York, NY: John Wiley & Sons, 1979.

Hall, Donald. *Writing Well.* Boston, MA: Little Brown, 1976.

Hodges, John. *Harbrace College Handbook.* San Diego, CA: Harcourt Brace Jovanovich, 1986.

Kessler, Lauren and Duncan McDonald. *When Words Collide.* Belmont, CA: Wadsworth Publishing Company, 1988.

Poe, Roy. *The McGraw-Hill Guide to Effective Business Reports.* New York, NY: McGraw-Hill, 1983.

Poe, Roy. *The McGraw-Hill Handbook of Business Letters.* New York, NY: McGraw-Hill, 1983.

Schell, John and John Stratton. *Writing on the Job.* New York, NY: New American Library, 1984.

Strunk, William, Jr. and E.B. White. *The Elements of Style.* New York, NY: Macmillan, 1959.

Williams, Joseph. *Style: Ten Lessons in Clarity and Grace.* New York, NY: Scott Foresman, 1985.

Zinsser, William. *On Writing Well.* New York, NY: Harper & Row, 1976.

Glossary of Terms

Acronym. A word formed from the first letters in a title or the first letters in a group of words: "AIDS" is an acronym for "Acquired Immune Deficiency Syndrome."

Active Verb. An active verb tells us that the subject of the sentence is doing the action. "John *hit* the ball." John is the subject; John is doing the action.

Adjective. A word that modifies or helps describe a noun. "John used the *large* bat."

Adverb. A word that modifies a verb, an adjective or another adverb.

- "John ran fast." The word "fast" modifies the verb "ran."
- "John ran *really* fast." The word "really" modifies the adverb "fast."
- "John is surprisingly devilish when he's not playing baseball." The word "surprisingly" modifies the adjective "devilish."

Apostrophe. A sign (') used to indicate letters that are left out of a word (can't), to show possession (The *dog's* bone.), or to show the plurals of abbreviations (Several *Ph.D.'s* met in the corner.).

Comma. The sign (,) used to indicate division in a sentence (Mary is a chemist, and John is a librarian.), to separate items in a list (John returned with apples, oranges and grapes.), to mark off thousands in numerals (1,582), and to separate types of information in bibliographical data (Brattleboro, Vermont: Amana Books, 1989).

Conjunction. A word used to connect words or groups of words.

- "John *and* Mary." The conjunction "and" connects the words "John" and "Mary."
- "Benjamin Franklin tells us to write things worth doing *or* do things worth writing." The conjunction "or" connects the groups of words "write things worth doing" and "do things worth writing."

Cliche. A word or expression that has lost its power through overuse. "Strong as an ox" is one example. Others include:

- "Pursuant to . . . "
- "In reference to your letter of . . . "
- "As per your request . . . "
- "Enclosed herewith please find . . ."

Contraction. The shortened form of a word ("can't" for "cannot") or a group of words ("I'm" for "I am").

Euphemism. The substitution of a mild, vague or general word for one considered too direct, harsh or blunt. "To pass away" is a euphemism for "to die."

Fragments. Words and phrases that cannot stand alone because they do not express complete thoughts. "As we lay awake listening to the river" is not a complete thought. Something has to follow to make this thought complete: "As we lay awake listening to the river, a bear appeared."

Gender. The three groups into which all English nouns fall: masculine, feminine and neuter.

Infinitive. The infinitive phrase is a verb with the word "to" in front of it: "to run," "to build," "to eat."

Jargon. The language that only someone in a particular trade, profession or group would ordinarily know: medical jargon, legal jargon, educational jargon, computer jargon.

Nouns. The names of people, places and things: Bob, New York, ball.

Passive Voice. Passive voice is when some action is being done to the subject of a sentence: "The ball *was hit by* John." "Ball" is the subject; the action is being done to the ball.

Prefix. Literally: something that comes before something else. In grammatical constructions: a group of letters that contain meaning and are placed before a root word to form a new word:

- prefix "un" + root "kind" = "unkind"
- prefix "pre" + root "figure" = "prefigure"

Prepositions. Prepositions show the relationship between two other words in a sentence: "Michael Harrington, 35, of 19 High Street, in Birmingham, was shot yesterday as he drove over the section of I-65 currently under construction." Some common prepositions are:

above	across	after	against	along
among	around	at	before	behind
below	beside	by	except	for
in	into	near	of	off
on	outside	over	through	to
toward	under	until	up	upon
with	within	without		

Suffix. Literally: something that follows something else. In grammatical construction: a group of letters containing meaning that are added to the end of a root word to form a new word:

- root "kind" + suffix "ly" = kindly
- root "strike" + suffix "ing" = striking

Run-ons. Too many sentences improperly joined. Sentences must be written separately, or they must be separated by a semicolon, or they must be joined by a conjunction ("and," "but," "nor"). Examples:

- Run-on: Mike was a poet he was also a critic.
- Correct: Mike was a poet; he was also a critic.

Sentence. A complete thought.

Syntax. The way words are put together in a phrase or sentence.

Verbs. Words that express some kind of action or state of being:

- Action: "John won the contest."
- State: "John is overweight."

Index

Buy two, get one free!

Each of our handbook series (LIFESTYLE, COMMUNICATION, PRODUCTIVITY, and LEADERSHIP) was designed to give you the most comprehensive collection of hands-on desktop references all related to a specific topic. They're a great value at the regular price of $12.95 ($14.95 in Canada); plus, at the unbeatable offer of buy two at the regular price and get one free, you can't find a better value in learning resources. **To order**, see the back of this page for the entire handbook selection.

1. Fill out and send the entire page by mail to:

    National Press Publications
    6901 West 63rd Street
    P.O. Box 2949
    Shawnee Mission, Kansas 66201-1349

2. Or **FAX 1-913-432-0824**

3. Or call toll-free **1-800-258-7248** (**1-800-685-4142** in Canada)

Fill out completely:

Name _____

Organization _____

Address _____

City _____

State/Province _____ ZIP/Postal Code _____

Telephone ( ) _____

Method of Payment:

❑ Enclosed is my check or money order

❑ Please charge to:

    ❑ MasterCard   ❑ VISA   ❑ American Express

Signature _____ Exp. Date _____

Credit Card Number

❑ ❑ ❑ ❑ ❑ ❑ ❑ ❑ ❑ ❑ ❑ ❑ ❑ ❑

To order multiple copies for co-workers and friends: U.S.   Can.

   20-50 copies $8.50 $10.95

   More than 50 copies ....$7.50 $ 9.95

VIP# 705-008414-092

OTHER DESKTOP HANDBOOKS

	Qty	Item#	Title	U.S.	Can.	Total
LEADERSHIP		410	The Supervisor's Handbook, Revised and Expanded	$12.95	$14.95	
		418	Total Quality Management	$12.95	$14.95	
		421	Change: Coping with Tomorrow Today	$12.95	$14.95	
		458	Positive Performance Management *A Guide to Win-Win Reviews*	$12.95	$14.95	
		459	Techniques of Successful Delegation	$12.95	$14.95	
		463	Powerful Leadership Skills for Women	$12.95	$14.95	
		494	Team-Building	$12.95	$14.95	
		495	How to Manage Conflict	$12.95	$14.95	
		469	Peak Performance	$12.95	$14.95	
COMMUNICATION		413	Dynamic Communication Skills for Women	$12.95	$14.95	
		414	The Write Stuff: *A Style Manual for Effective Business Writing*	$12.95	$14.95	
		417	Listen Up: *Hear What's Really Being Said*	$12.95	$14.95	
		442	Assertiveness: *Get What You Want Without Being Pushy*	$12.95	$14.95	
		460	Techniques to Improve Your Writing Skills	$12.95	$14.95	
		461	Powerful Presentation Skills	$12.95	$14.95	
		482	Techniques of Effective Telephone Communication	$12.95	$14.95	
		485	Personal Negotiating Skills	$12.95	$14.95	
		488	Customer Service: *The Key to Winning Lifetime Customers*	$12.95	$14.95	
		498	How to Manage Your Boss	$12.95	$14.95	
PRODUCTIVITY		411	Getting Things Done: *An Achiever's Guide to Time Management*	$12.95	$14.95	
		443	A New Attitude	$12.95	$14.95	
		468	Understanding the Bottom Line: *Finance for the Non-Financial Manager*	$12.95	$14.95	
		483	Successful Sales Strategies: *A Woman's Perspective*	$12.95	$14.95	
		489	Doing Business Over the Phone *Telemarketing for the '90s*	$12.95	$14.95	
		496	Motivation & Goal-Setting *The Keys to Achieving Success*	$12.95	$14.95	
LIFESTYLE		415	Balancing Career & Family: *Overcoming the Superwoman Syndrome*	$12.95	$14.95	
		416	Real Men Don't Vacuum	$12.95	$14.95	
		464	Self-Esteem: *The Power to Be Your Best*	$12.95	$14.95	
		484	The Stress Management Handbook	$12.95	$14.95	
		486	Parenting: *Ward & June Don't Live Here Anymore*	$12.95	$14.95	
		487	How to Get the Job You Want	$12.95	$14.95	

SALES TAX All purchases subject to state and local sales tax. Questions? Call **1-800-258-7248**		
Subtotal		
Sales Tax **(Add appropriate state and local tax)**		
Shipping and Handling **($1 one item, 50¢ each additional item)**		
Total		

VIP# 705-008414-092